PICKERS IS A THIEF

A Story About Shoplifting

Written & Illustrated by

GARY D. ANTILLA

An *At-Risk Stories Series* Book
For Ages 9-12

ABOUT THE AUTHOR

Gary D. Antilla is a guidance counselor in Green Bay, Wisconsin. A former sixth-grade teacher, he developed the idea for *Pickers* after working for 15 years as a part-time security person in a department store. Gary received both his B.S. and M.A. from Northern Michigan University. He is married to Jane and the father of two children, Angela and David, to whom he dedicates this book.

Published by
mar∗co products, inc.
1443 Old York Road, Warminster, PA 18974
1-800-448-2197

Library of Congress Catalog Card Number: 96-079868

ISBN: 1-57543-027-4

Printed in the U.S.A.

PICKERS IS A THIEF

HI! MY NAME IS PICKERS and I'd like to tell you a story. It's not really a happy story, but I want to share it so you can do something I wasn't good at—thinking before doing something, rather than being sorry after it was done.

My family was an ordinary family, probably something like yours. Mom and Dad were always proud of me, but they never knew what I was like when they weren't around. I'm not saying I was real bad, but I was always the one who did things on a dare. You know, like ringing doorbells and hiding, or throwing a rock through the window of an old house.

Well, it wasn't long before I started taking things around the house that didn't belong to me. Nobody missed the stuff I took, and it became kind of fun to do. The worst thing was that it became a habit that I just couldn't break. I started getting into bigger things, like Mom's money that she kept in the cookie jar. Can you guess what happened? That's right! I got caught one day with my hand in the cookie jar.

My mom told my dad, and he had a long talk with me when he got home from work. He also yelled quite a bit. I was grounded to my room for the next few weeks, and I couldn't have any friends over to play or visit. You'd think I would have learned my lesson from this, because I felt guilty every time Mom was nice to me.

I guess getting caught did stop me from taking things from my parents, but now I was sneaking around the neighborhood taking things. I got to be quite good at it. At least I thought I was good, because I never got caught. The only thing I began to notice was that no parents wanted me to come over to their houses or let their kids play with me. But I didn't care because I had a lot of friends at school.

Speaking of school, my habit even began to grow while I was there. On the way home one afternoon, I was walking across the playground with a few friends. We found a couple of bats and balls that belonged to the school. I had given up some friends, but I wouldn't give up those bats and balls.

I began to be very brave about taking things from others at school. I could sneak things out of the kids' and teacher's desks without them even knowing I did it.

It wasn't long before I was taking just anything. It became fun to see if I could get away with it. It got so bad that I didn't know where to hide the stuff. My desk and locker were both packed to the top, and I didn't dare take my loot home.

One day, the teacher decided to have a desk and locker check. I didn't know what to do! I said that my desk and locker were mine and nobody had the right to go into them. All the kids looked at me and wondered why I was making such a fuss over this. The teacher didn't stop. She started going through the desks and went from one to another until she came to mine. Can you imagine what I felt like when she opened mine?

You would think my story would have ended by this time, but it didn't. I guess nothing really bad had happened yet. My teacher called my parents. I was grounded again. This time I was grounded for a very long time and lost all my TV privileges. I felt about as low as a worm, but I still hadn't learned my lesson.

One day, a bunch of kids were talking and bragging about how easy it was to rip-off (take things) from one of the department stores. The next Saturday, we all went to the store. Everyone took something except my best friend and me. It was so easy that it made me angry to see that my best friend and I had been left out.

If not having anything wasn't bad enough, the others began to tease us. Well, you know me! I never pass up a dare. I talked my best friend into going back into the store. I worked it out so that I would take the things and my best friend could be the lookout. I took some miniature racing cars and a cassette tape. I didn't really want either of them, but they were small and easy to hide. My friend just stood nearby and watched to see if anyone would notice.

We were just outside the door when I heard a voice behind me say, "Didn't you forget to do something?" I didn't know what to do. I was going to run, but there he was, as big as a building and looking down at me. I WAS CAUGHT!

He took us to a place in the store called a security office. He told me I was being held for shoplifting and asked me to empty my pockets. I began to cry and said I didn't know how the cars and the tape got into my pockets. My story didn't matter to him. He just kept on writing on his forms.

He wanted to know why I had done it, and I couldn't give him an answer. I finally said that the store wouldn't miss what I had taken anyway. That answer made him very upset. He said it did make a difference. The store has to pay for everything in it, and when something is stolen, the store loses money. He told me that when the store loses money it has to charge higher prices and honest people have to pay more for what they buy because of people like me.

By this time, I was scared silly. My best friend was crying and wanted to go home. The security man said my friend was going to the police station with me because he was an accomplice. (That's someone who is guilty because he or she helped someone else do something wrong.) My best friend really didn't take anything and I felt bad because I talked him into coming with me.

It wasn't long before a police officer came in and said we had to go down to the police station. I begged him not to take us, but he didn't listen. He just said that we were going, and I was going to be arrested for shoplifting. He walked us right through the center of the store and put handcuffs on us so we wouldn't run. Everybody was laughing and pointing at us. I guess you know how we felt!

On the way to the police station, I could just picture in my mind what was going to happen. I could see myself in a cell and my mom and dad walking in to get me. A million questions ran through my mind. How could I ever look at them? What was I going to say? Would they ever love me again?

At the police station my friend and I were separated. A police officer showed me around the place. He told me I was going to have a criminal record until I was 18 years old. My parents were called, and I heard the police officer tell them they were going to have to go to court with me. Before my parents came, the police officer took me to the jail and told me to take a good look around. Then he asked me, “Is this where you want to end up?” I was too scared to answer him. In fact, I started to cry. I guess he knew what my answer was.

Just about then, my parents arrived. I began to cry even louder, but I could tell by my Mom's red eyes that it wasn't going to help. I finally knew then that I would never do anything like that again. I could just see all the hurt and bad feelings in the room, and I knew I had caused them.

Well, boys and girls, that's my story. I hurt the people who loved me most and I hurt myself. You are still young enough to make some good choices. But, please, be sure you do something that I took too long to learn—

THINK BEFORE YOU DO SOMETHING, NOT AFTER!

QUESTIONS TO ASK YOURSELF

Now that you have read the story, ask yourself these questions. The answers are on the next page.

1. What was Pickers' problem?

2. Who did Pickers hurt?

3. Why do you think Pickers did these things?

4. Did Pickers seem to know that stealing was a problem?

5. How do you think Pickers' parents felt?

6. Why did Pickers steal?

7. Would you want Pickers for a friend?

8. How could Pickers have helped himself?

ANSWERS TO PAGE 13

1. Pickers' problem was stealing. It eventually became a habit.
2. Pickers hurt his parents, his friends and himself.
3. Stealing became a habit. Pickers never thought about the consequences.
4. Pickers realized the problem at the end of the story when he was taken to the police station and saw the reaction on his parents' faces.
5. Pickers' parents were disappointed, upset, angry, embarrassed, etc.
6. Pickers stole because he did not think before acting.
7. You probably would not want Pickers for a friend because you would not know when he would get you in trouble or even steal from you.
8. Pickers needs to learn to think before acting.